Print Handwriting WORKBOOK
For Kids Ages 8 - 12

This Workbook Belongs To:

_____

Copyright Notice
Print Handwriting Workbook For Kids Ages 8-12
©2025, BrainWave Books
All rights reserved.
No part of this book may be copied, reproduced, distributed, or transmitted in any form or by any means, including photocopying, recording, or other electronic or mechanical methods, without the prior written permission of the publisher, except in the case of brief quotations for review purposes as permitted by copyright law.
This workbook is for personal, educational, and non-commercial use only. Schools, educators, and parents may use this material for individual instruction but may not reproduce or distribute copies for multiple students or commercial purposes without permission.
Unauthorized resale, reproduction, or distribution of this book, in whole or in part, in print, digital, or any other format, is strictly prohibited. Violators may be subject to legal action.

Thank You For Choosing BrainWave Books!

Hi there!

We're so glad you picked up this book. BrainWave Books is a small, family-run brand—just the two of us, a husband and wife team—creating educational books that our own kids love and learn from. We know how important it is to have quality learning resources, and we're dedicated to making books that truly help learners of all ages.

Since we're a small team, we're always looking to improve. **Your feedback—whether big or small—helps us create better books for you and others like you.** If you have any thoughts, ideas, or suggestions, we'd love to hear them!

You can share your feedback by scanning the QR code below. We read every message and use your input to make our books better.

Thanks again for being part of our journey! We hope you enjoy this book as much as we enjoyed creating it.

— The BrainWave Books Team

Welcome To Your Handwriting Journey

Handwriting is an essential skill that plays an important role in everyday life. Whether you are writing notes for school, completing assignments, filling out forms, or simply jotting down ideas, the ability to write neatly and legibly helps ensure that your words are clear and easy to read. While technology has made typing more common, handwriting remains a fundamental skill that strengthens brain function, improves focus, and enhances communication.

Studies have shown that writing by hand helps with memory and learning, making it easier to retain information compared to typing. Well-formed letters and proper spacing allow for faster and more efficient writing, preventing frustration when reading back notes or written work. In school, neat handwriting can also help ensure that teachers and classmates can easily read your work, reducing the chance of mistakes or misunderstandings.

Beyond academics, good handwriting builds confidence. When your writing is clear and polished, it reflects care and attention to detail, showing that you take pride in your work. Whether you are writing a personal letter, filling out an application, or creating a list, strong handwriting skills will benefit you for years to come.

This workbook is designed to help you refine your handwriting through structured practice and engaging exercises. You will begin with a quick review of letters, progress to writing words, move on to sentence practice, and ultimately work on writing complete paragraphs. Along the way, you will find fun content such as jokes, riddles, and interesting facts to keep the exercises enjoyable.

Improving handwriting takes patience and regular practice, but the results are worth the effort. Work at your own pace, focus on forming each letter carefully, and most importantly— enjoy the process!

Handwriting Tips And Best Practices

Before beginning the exercises, it is important to establish good writing habits. The following tips will help you write neatly and comfortably:

Proper Pencil Grip
Hold your pencil using the **tripod grip**, where your thumb and index finger grasp the pencil while the middle finger provides support underneath. A relaxed grip allows for better control and reduces hand fatigue. Holding the pencil too tightly can cause discomfort and make writing more difficult.

Posture & Paper Positioning
Sit with **both feet flat on the floor** and rest your writing arm comfortably on the table. Good posture prevents strain and helps with better letter control.

Position your paper at a slight angle for better movement:

- Right-handed writers should tilt the top left corner slightly upward.
- Left-handed writers should tilt the top right corner slightly upward to prevent smudging.

Letter Spacing & Consistency
- Write letters at a **consistent size** to maintain readability. Letters that are too large or too small can make writing look uneven.

- Keep a **steady slant**—letters should lean slightly in the same direction or remain upright.

- Leave **appropriate spacing between words**. Words placed too closely together can be difficult to read, while excessive spacing can make sentences appear disjointed.

Common Handwriting Mistakes And How to Fix Them

- **Irregular letter sizing:** Use the provided handwriting lines to maintain uniform letter height.

- **Floating or misplaced letters:** Ensure that the base of each letter sits on the baseline.

- **Writing too quickly:** Slow down to maintain control and accuracy in letter formation.

- **Inconsistent spacing between words:** Leave equal space between words so they don't run together or appear too far apart. A good rule of thumb is to leave enough space for the tip of your pinky finger between words.

- **Letters slanting in different directions:** Keep letters tilted in the same direction (either upright or slightly slanted) to make writing more uniform and readable.

- **Grip too tight or too loose:** Holding the pencil too tightly can cause hand fatigue, while too loose can lead to shaky writing. Use a comfortable, relaxed grip for better control.

- **Uneven pressure on the pencil:** Pressing too hard can make writing messy and difficult to erase, while too light can be hard to read. Aim for a steady, even pressure on the pencil.

- **Letters not fully formed:** Make sure every letter is complete, with proper strokes and loops, so they don't look like a different letter.

With time and effort, these small adjustments will lead to **smoother, clearer, and more consistent handwriting.**

Table of Contents

1. LETTERS
Tracing (A-Z) 1-13
Alphabet Maze 14-15
Match the Letter Styles 16-19

2. WORDS
Tracing Words 20-45
Word Builder Game 46-49

3. SENTENCES
Jokes 50-63
Sentence Scramble 64-65
Inspirational Sentences 66-77
Sentence Scramble 78-79
Fun Facts 80-94
Creative Lettering Challenge 95-102

4. PRACTICAL WRITING APPLICATIONS
My To-Do List 103
Grocery List 104
Friendly Letter 105
Party Invitation 106
Short Biography 107
Directions to a Location 108
Short Advertisement 109
Filling Out a Simple Form 110
Weather Report 111

Table of Contents

    Movie/TV Show Review 112
    Breaking News 113
    Speech/Announcement 114
    Complete the Story 115-120

5. WRITING PROMPTS

    If You Could Have Any Superpower 121
    A Mysterious Door Appears 122
    If You Could Visit Any Time in History 123
    The Day Animals Started Talking 124
    A New Planet Has Been Discovered! 125
    Your Dream Amusement Park 126
    If You Could Switch Lives with a Book or Movie Character 127
    The Best Invention Ever! 128

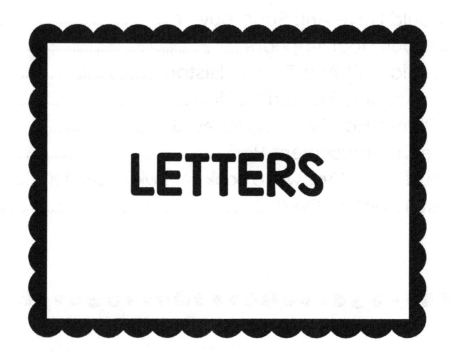

A a B b

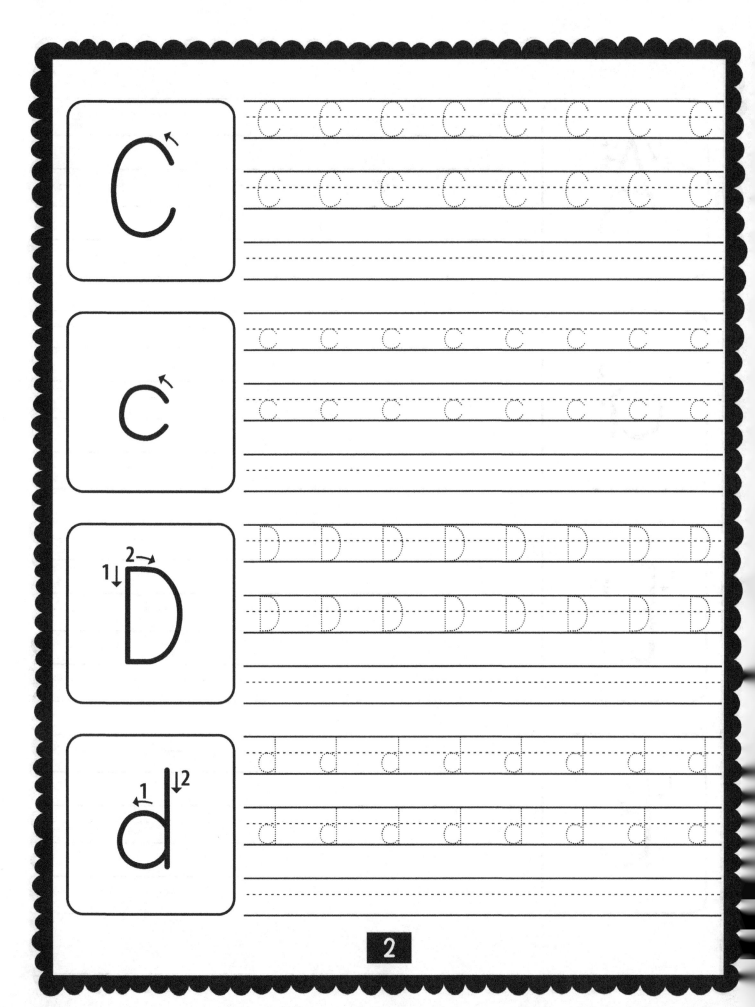

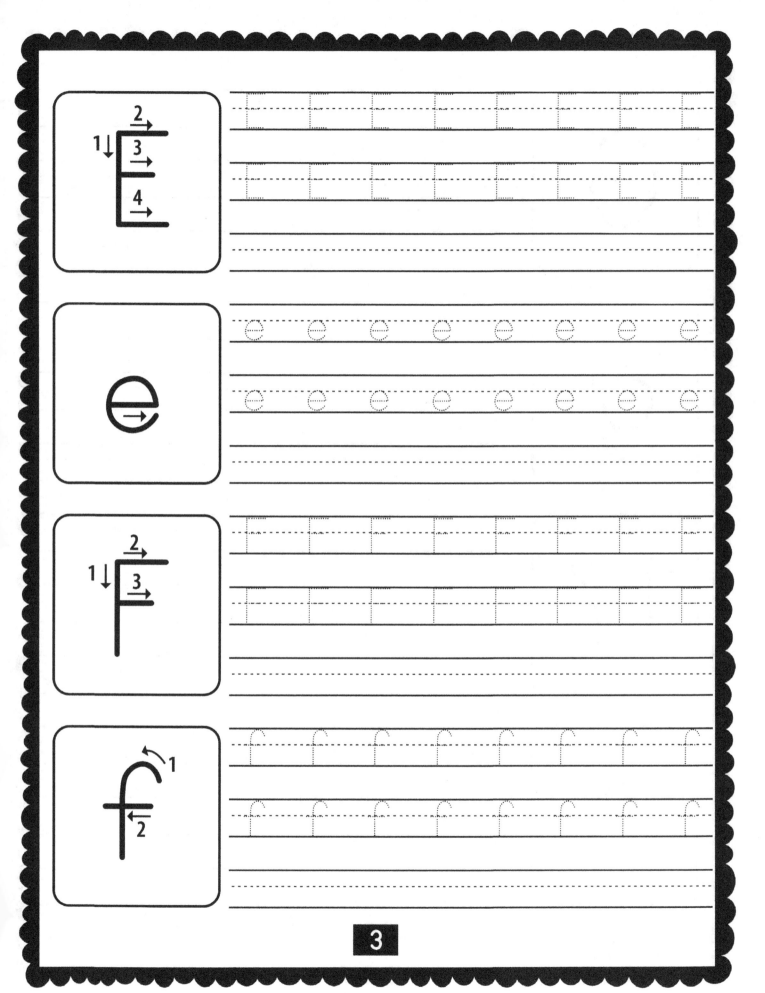

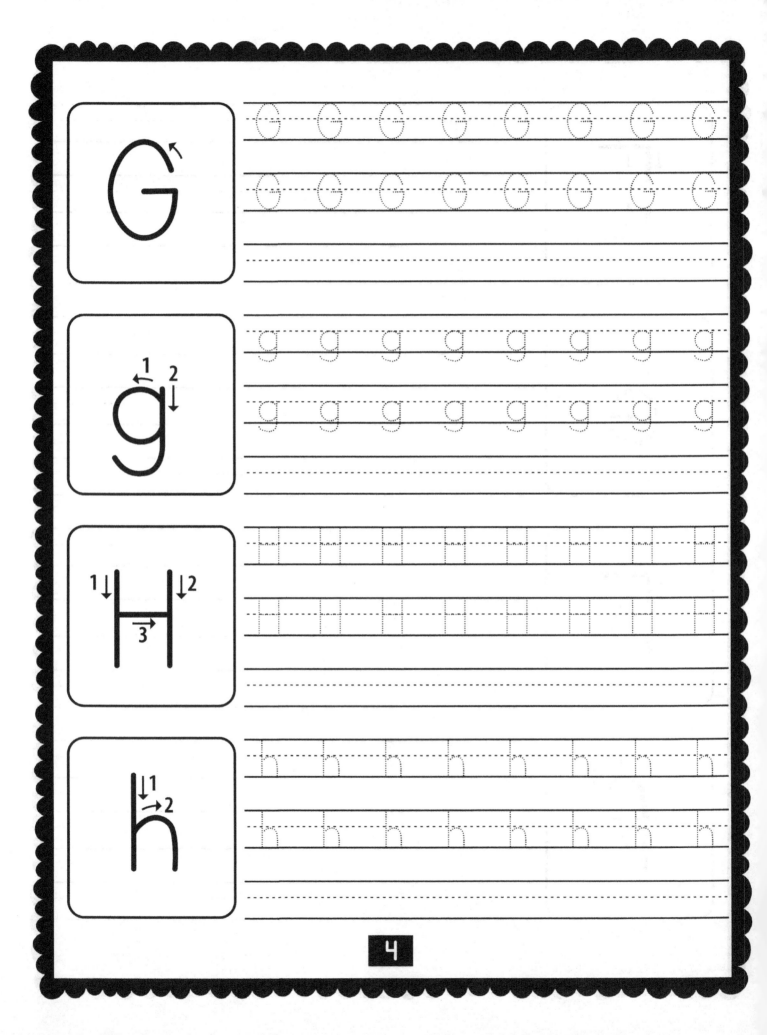

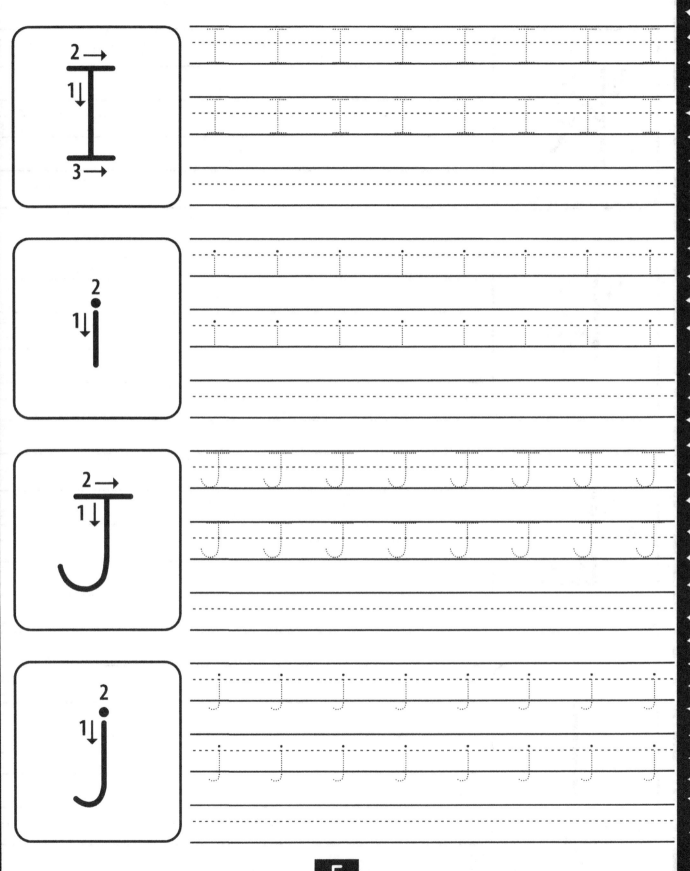

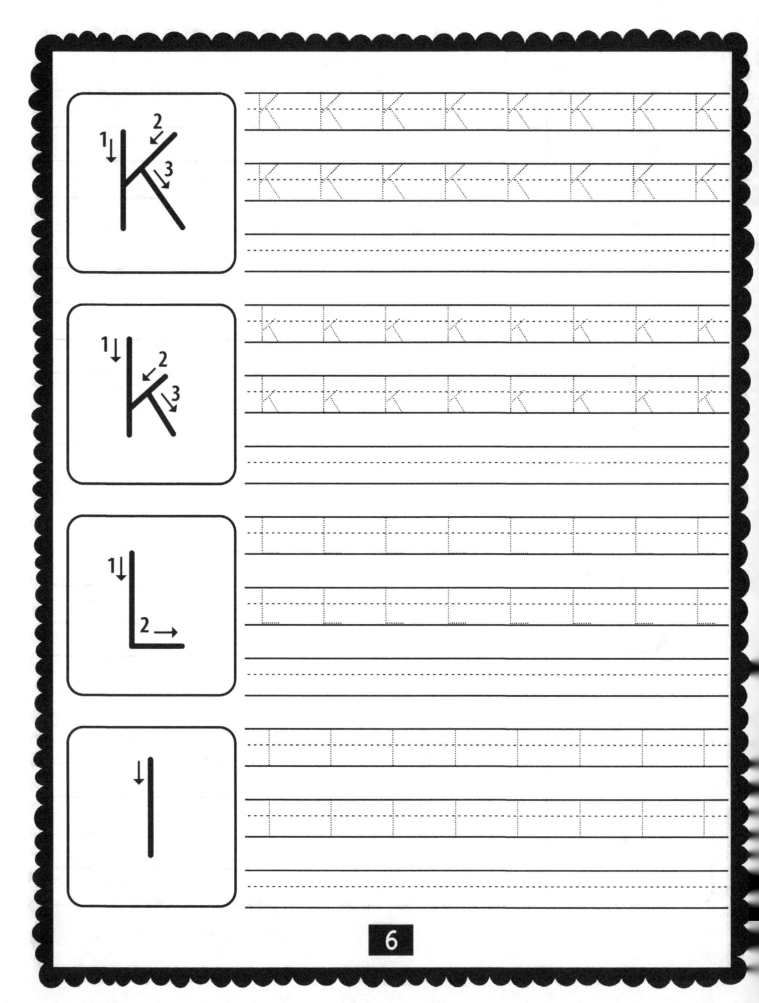

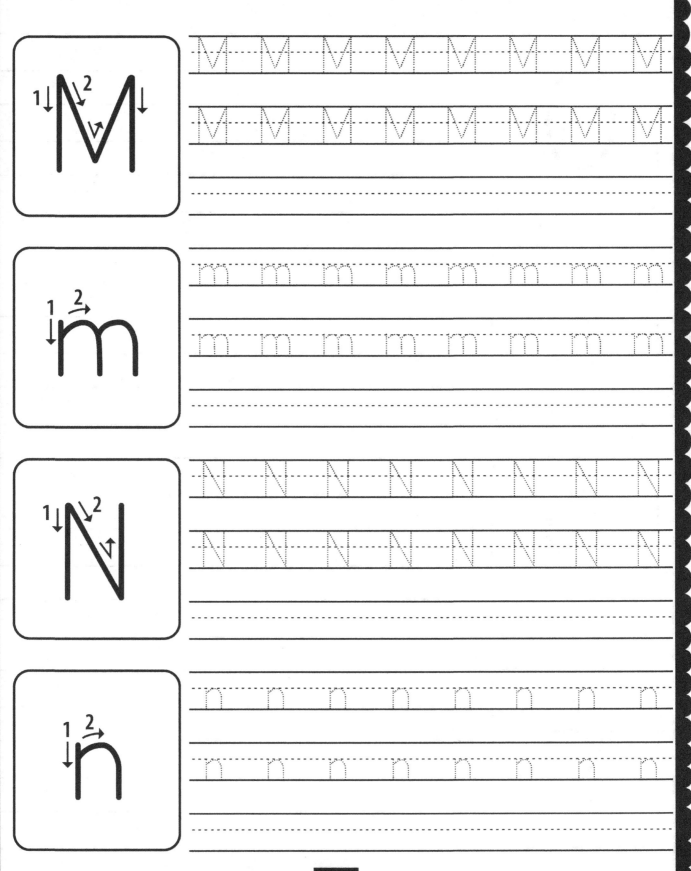

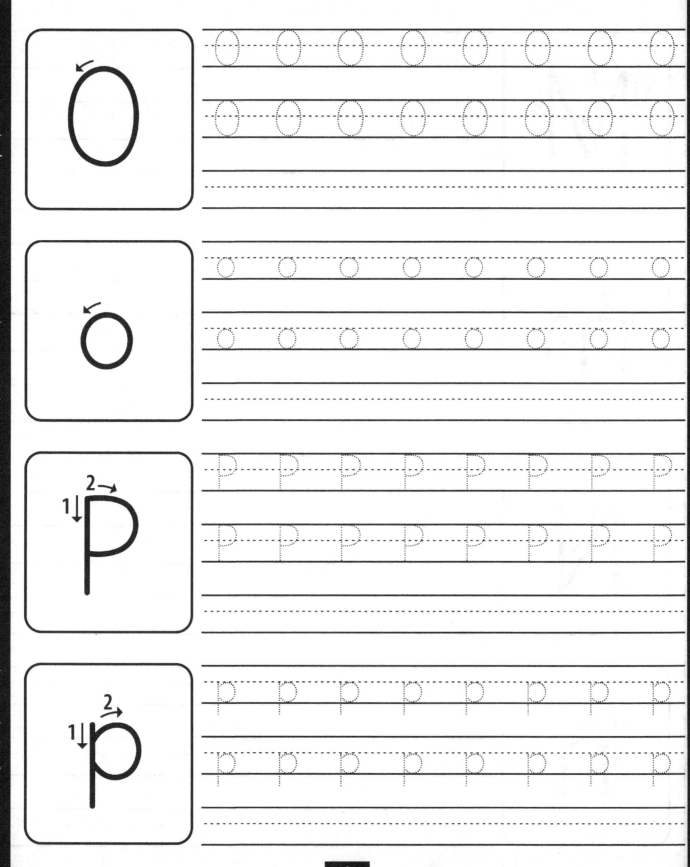

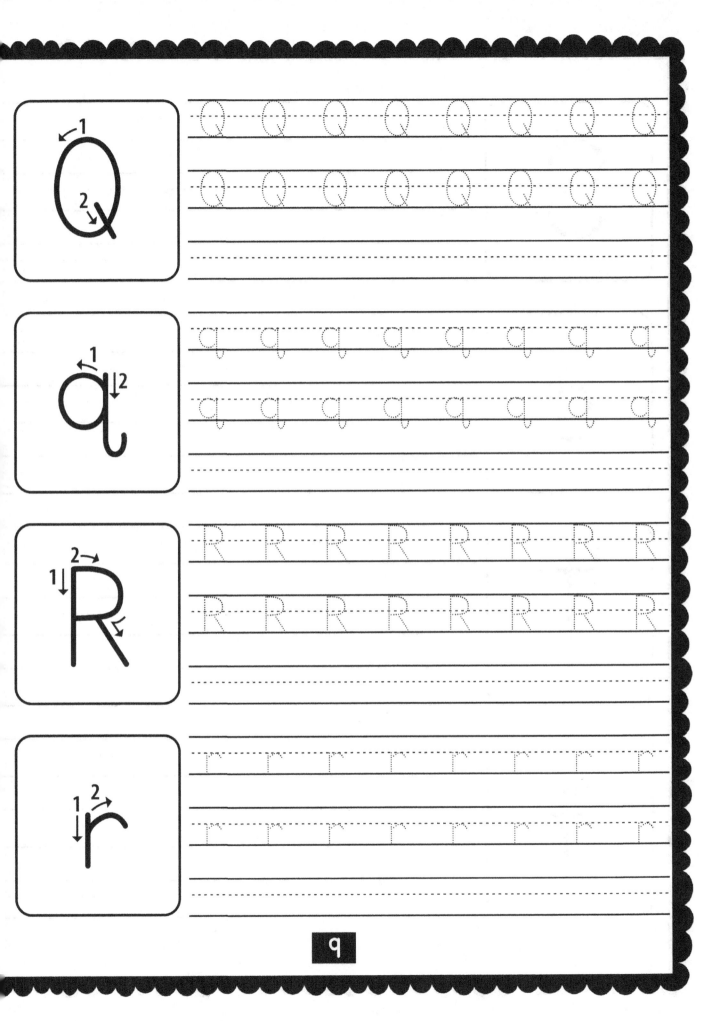

S

s

T

t

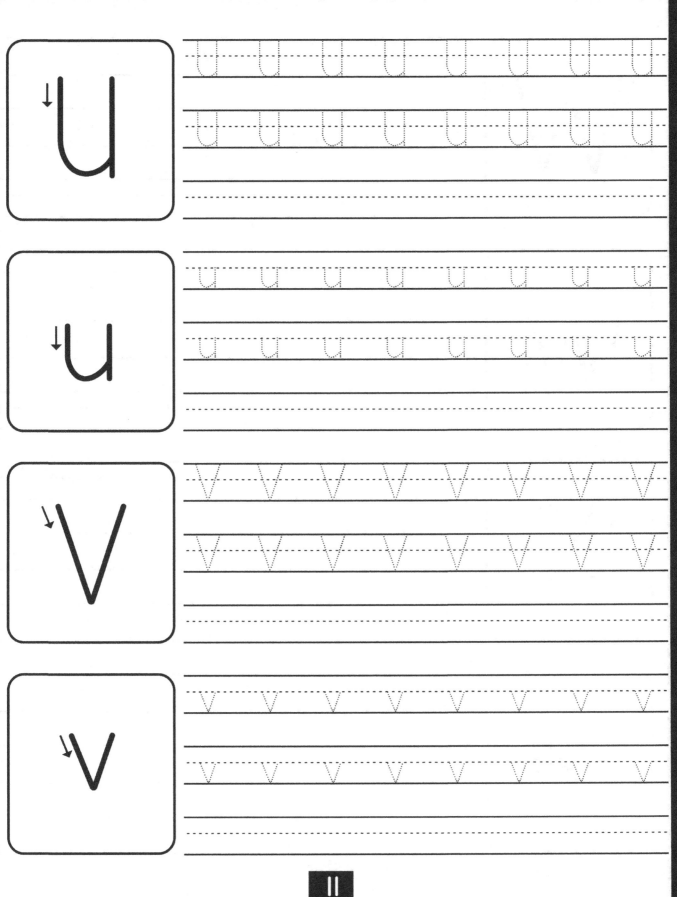

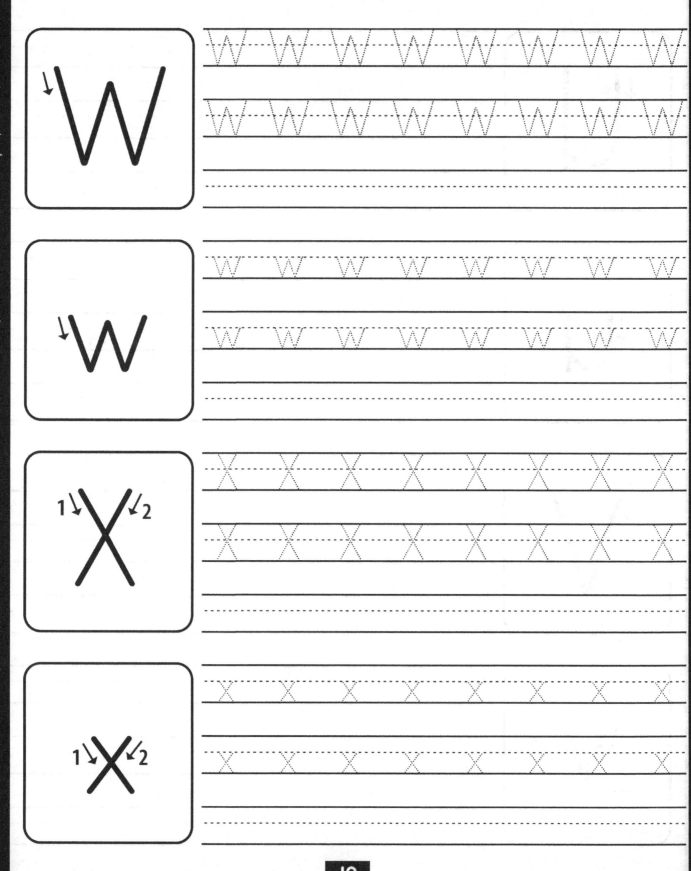

13

ALPHABET MAZE

Instructions: Start at A and trace your way through, following the letters in alphabetical order until you reach Z.

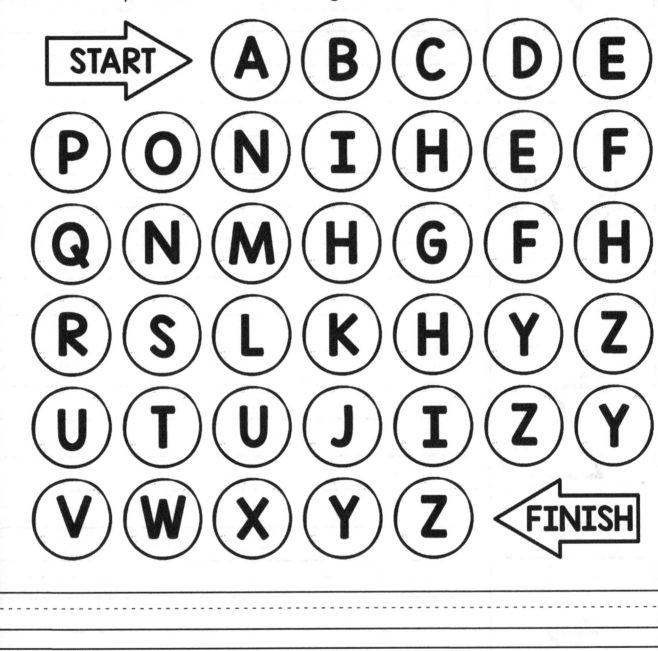

ALPHABET MAZE

Instructions: Start at a and trace your way through, following the letters in alphabetical order until you reach z.

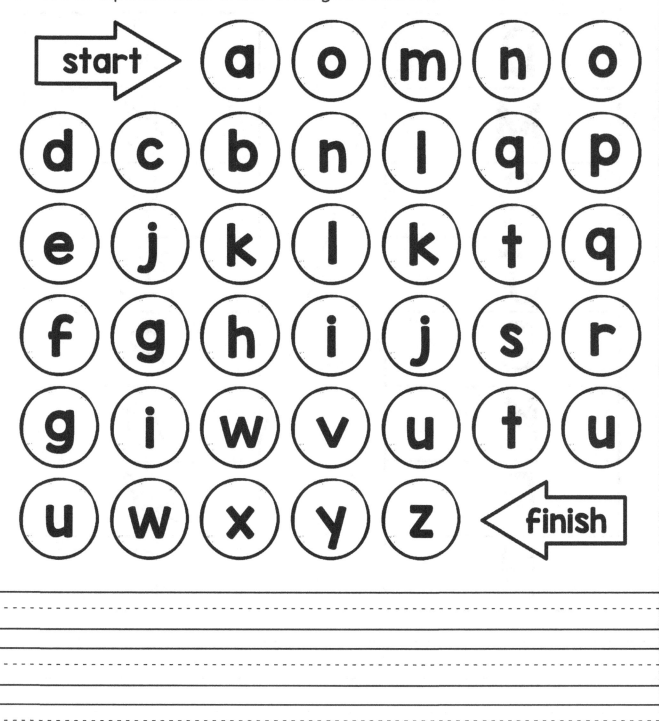

MATCH THE LETTER STYLES

PRINT LETTERS	CURSIVE LETTERS
D	J
M	K
Q	H
J	M
S	P
K	D
P	S
H	Q

MATCH THE LETTER STYLES

PRINT LETTERS	CURSIVE LETTERS
f	o
o	u
c	w
y	y
r	h
u	c
b	r
w	f

17

MATCH THE LETTER STYLES

PRINT LETTERS	FANCY LETTERS
X	R
A	C
R	L
G	X
C	W
W	G
L	E
E	A

18

MATCH THE LETTER STYLES

PRINT LETTERS	FANCY LETTERS
v	*i*
d	*q*
q	*t*
i	*n*
h	*d*
t	*z*
z	*v*
n	*h*

Apple   Apple   Apple   Apple

Andy   Andy   Andy   Andy

Amazing   Amazing   Amazing

allowed   allowed   allowed

airplane   airplane   airplane

artistic   artistic   artistic

Belly   Belly   Belly   Belly

Blake   Blake   Blake   Blake

Banana   Banana   Banana

bounce   bounce   bounce

breeze   breeze   breeze

butterfly   butterfly   butterfly

Camp   Camp   Camp   Camp

Count   Count   Count   Count

Captain   Captain   Captain

chocolate   chocolate   chocolate

clever   clever   clever

cheerful   cheerful   cheerful

Dazzle   Dazzle   Dazzle   Dazzle

Drink   Drink   Drink   Drink

Dinosaur   Dinosaur   Dinosaur

dreamer   dreamer   dreamer

delight   delight   delight

dribble   dribble   dribble

Echo   Echo   Echo   Echo

Enjoy   Enjoy   Enjoy   Enjoy

Elephant   Elephant   Elephant

exciting   exciting   exciting

energy   energy   energy

explore   explore   explore

Fizzy   Fizzy   Fizzy   Fizzy

Fancy   Fancy   Fancy   Fancy

Fireworks   Fireworks   Fireworks

friendly   friendly   friendly

fortune   fortune   fortune

flutter   flutter   flutter

Gallon   Gallon   Gallon   Gallon

Greg   Greg   Greg   Greg

Giggle   Giggle   Giggle   Giggle

glitter   glitter   glitter   glitter

grateful   grateful   grateful

galaxy   galaxy   galaxy   galaxy

Happy   Happy   Happy   Happy

Hug   Hug   Hug   Hug

Hope   Hope   Hope   Hope

harmony   harmony   harmony

hilarious   hilarious   hilarious

humming   humming   humming

Ignite Ignite Ignite Ignite

Iceland Iceland Iceland

Inventor Inventor Inventor

iguana iguana iguana

imagine imagine imagine

inspire inspire inspire

July   July   July   July

Jump   Jump   Jump   Jump

Joy   Joy   Joy   Joy

jungle   jungle   jungle

jigsaw   jigsaw   jigsaw

jamming   jamming   jamming

Koala   Koala   Koala   Koala

King   King   King   King

Kick   Kick   Kick   Kick

knight   knight   knight   knight

kangaroo   kangaroo   kangaroo

kindness   kindness   kindness

Live   Live   Live   Live

Lake   Lake   Lake   Lake

Lucky   Lucky   Lucky   Lucky

legend   legend   legend   legend

lollipop   lollipop   lollipop

laughter   laughter   laughter

March   March   March   March

Magic   Magic   Magic   Magic

Mellow   Mellow   Mellow   Mellow

munch   munch   munch   munch

marshmallow   marshmallow

mystery   mystery   mystery

Nature   Nature   Nature   Nature

Nutty   Nutty   Nutty   Nutty

Norway   Norway   Norway

never   never   never   never

nowhere   nowhere   nowhere

notebook   notebook   notebook

Over   Over   Over   Over

Oops   Oops   Oops   Oops

Orbit   Orbit   Orbit   Orbit

outshine   outshine   outshine

octopus   octopus   octopus

omelette   omelette   omelette

Penny   Penny   Penny   Penny

Puppy   Puppy   Puppy   Puppy

Pirate   Pirate   Pirate   Pirate

paddle   paddle   paddle   paddle

poppy   poppy   poppy   poppy

pluck   pluck   pluck   pluck

Queen Queen Queen Queen

Quinn Quinn Quinn Quinn

Quest Quest Quest Quest

quick quick quick quick

quirky quirky quirky quirky

quiver quiver quiver quiver

Ride   Ride   Ride   Ride

Rachel   Rachel   Rachel   Rachel

Rocket   Rocket   Rocket   Rocket

rainbow   rainbow   rainbow

rooster   rooster   rooster

reverse   reverse   reverse

Sunny   Sunny   Sunny   Sunny

Silly   Silly   Silly   Silly

Swoosh   Swoosh   Swoosh

superhero   superhero   superhero

sprinkle   sprinkle   sprinkle

slowly   slowly   slowly   slowly

Tickle   tickle   tickle   tickle

Treasure   Treasure   Treasure

Tornado   Tornado   Tornado

twinkle   twinkle   twinkle

tumble   tumble   tumble

teapot   teapot   teapot

Uplift   Uplift   Uplift   Uplift

Unique   Unique   Unique   Unique

Umbrella   Umbrella   Umbrella

universe   universe   universe

unicorn   unicorn   unicorn

upbeat   upbeat   upbeat

Very   Very   Very   Very

Velvet   Velvet   Velvet   Velvet

Victory   Victory   Victory

vacation   vacation   vacation

vibrant   vibrant   vibrant

volcano   volcano   volcano

Wild   Wild   Wild   Wild

Wiggle   Wiggle   Wiggle   Wiggle

Whistle   Whistle   Whistle

whimsy   whimsy   whimsy

wonderful   wonderful

wander   wander   wander

Xavier   Xavier   Xavier   Xavier

X-ray   X-ray   X-ray

X-factor   X-factor   X-factor

xylophone   xylophone   xylophone

example   example   example

extra   extra   extra   extra

Yearly   Yearly   Yearly   Yearly

Yellow   Yellow   Yellow   Yellow

Yodel   Yodel   Yodel   Yodel

yummy   yummy   yummy

yippee   yippee   yippee

yo - yo   yo - yo   yo - yo

Zebra　Zebra　Zebra　Zebra

Zest　Zest　Zest　Zest

Zoom　Zoom　Zoom　Zoom

zigzag　zigzag　zigzag　zigzag

zing　zing　zing　zing

zany　zany　zany　zany

WORD BUILDER GAME

Instructions: Use the letters inside the circle to build as many words as possible! You can use each letter only once per word.

I   N   T
R   A   E

1. rain
2. _____
3. _____
4. _____
5. _____
6. _____
7. _____
8. _____
9. _____
10. _____

Find the 6 Letter Word. _____

WORD BUILDER GAME

Instructions: Use the letters inside the circle to build as many words as possible! You can use each letter only once per word.

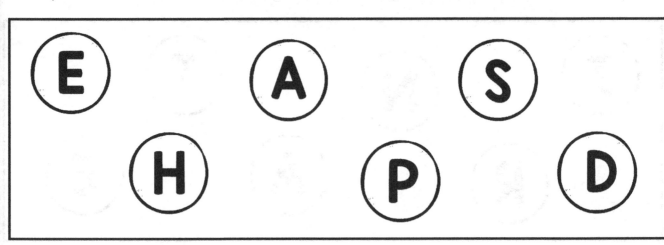

1. _____
2. _____
3. _____
4. _____
5. _____

6. _____
7. _____
8. _____
9. _____
10. _____

Find the 6 Letter Word. _____

WORD BUILDER GAME

Instructions: Use the letters inside the circle to build as many words as possible! You can use each letter only once per word.

N B L
 E   R   I

1. _____
2. _____
3. _____
4. _____
5. _____

6. _____
7. _____
8. _____
9. _____
10. _____

Find the 6 Letter Word. _____

48

WORD BUILDER GAME

Instructions: Use the letters inside the circle to build as many words as possible! You can use each letter only once per word.

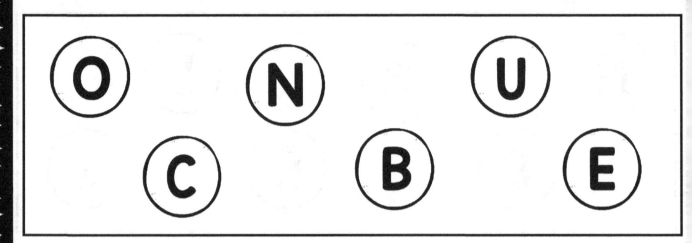

1. _____
2. _____
3. _____
4. _____
5. _____

6. _____
7. _____
8. _____
9. _____
10. _____

Find the 6 Letter Word. _____

SENTENCES

Instructions: Trace the sentence and then write it on your own.

Why did the scarecrow win an award? Because he was outstanding in his field.

What did one ocean say to the other ocean? Nothing, they just waved.

Instructions: Trace the sentence and then write it on your own.

Why can't your nose be 12 inches long? Because then it would be a foot.

Why don't skeletons fight each other? Because they don't have the guts.

Instructions: Trace the sentence and then write it on your own.

Why did the golfer bring an extra pair of pants? In case he got a hole in one.

What did the left eye say to the right eye? "Between us, something smells!"

Instructions: Trace the sentence and then write it on your own.

Why did the music teacher go to jail? Because she got caught with a sharp note.

Why did the banana go to the doctor? Because it wasn't peeling well.

Instructions: Trace the sentence and then write it on your own.

What do you call a bear with no teeth? A gummy bear.

Why did the math book look sad? Because it had too many problems.

Why did the football coach go to the bank? To get his quarterback.

Instructions: Trace the sentence and then write it on your own.

Why don't pirates take baths?
Because they just wash up on
shore.

What did the librarian say when
the books were late? I'm checking
you out.

Instructions: Trace the sentence and then write it on your own.

How do you know the ocean is friendly? It waves.

What's the best time to go to the dentist? Tooth-hurty.

What kind of room has no doors or windows? A mushroom.

Instructions: Trace the sentence and then write it on your own.

What did the big flower say to the little flower? "Hey, bud."

Why did the bicycle fall over? Because it was two-tired.

Why don't eggs tell jokes? Because they might crack up.

Instructions: Trace the sentence and then write it on your own.

What kind of tree fits in your hand? A palm tree.

What's the best way to throw a party on Mars? You planet.

Why did the cookie go to the doctor? Because it felt crumby.

Instructions: Trace the sentence and then write it on your own.

What's brown and sticky?
A stick.

What has hands but can't clap?
A clock.

What kind of shoes do ninjas wear? Sneakers

Instructions: Trace the sentence and then write it on your own.

Why did the chicken join a band?

Because it had the drumsticks.

What kind of key opens a banana?

A monkey.

Why do bees have sticky hair?

Because they use honeycombs.

Instructions: Trace the sentence and then write it on your own.

What do you call a sleeping bull?
A bulldozer.

What's orange and sounds like a parrot? A carrot.

What did one plate say to the other plate? Lunch is on me.

Instructions: Trace the sentence and then write it on your own.

Why did the pencil go to school? To get a little sharper.

What's black and white and read all over? A newspaper.

What do you call an alligator in a vest? An investigator.

Instructions: Trace the sentence and then write it on your own.

Why did the skeleton go to the party alone? Because he had no body to go with him.

SENTENCE SCRAMBLE

Instructions: Write the correct sentence neatly below each scrambled version.

- Scrambled: the playground ran across We

- Correct: _____

- Scrambled: has blue My very eyes sister

- Correct: _____

- Scrambled: food favorite pizza is My

- Correct: _____

- Scrambled: forgot school at I my backpack

- Correct: _____

SENTENCE SCRAMBLE

Instructions: Write the correct sentence neatly below each scrambled version.

- Scrambled: soccer loves My brother playing

- Correct: _____

- Scrambled: birthday balloons had ten My party

- Correct: _____

- Scrambled: dog chased little My squirrel a big

- Correct: _____

- Scrambled: watched last night movie a We scary

- Correct: _____

Instructions: Trace the sentence and then write it on your own.

Courage is not the absence of fear but the ability to move forward.

Strength doesn't come from what you can do-it comes from overcoming challenges.

Instructions: Trace the sentence and then write it on your own.

Believe in yourself, and you are halfway there.

Every great achievement starts with a single step.

You are capable of more than you know.

Instructions: Trace the sentence and then write it on your own.

Mistakes help you learn and grow stronger.

The harder you work, the greater your success.

A positive attitude can change your whole day.

Instructions: Trace the sentence and then write it on your own.

Great things take time-keep going.

Success comes to those who never give up.

You don't have to be perfect to be amazing.

Instructions: Trace the sentence and then write it on your own.

Every day is a new opportunity to do your best.

Believe in your dreams, and they will believe in you.

Be yourself. Everyone else is already taken.

Instructions: Trace the sentence and then write it on your own.

You can do anything if you set your mind to it.

The best way to predict the future is to create it.

Be the reason someone smiles today.

Instructions: Trace the sentence and then write it on your own.

Don't be afraid to stand out and be yourself.

Do what is right, even when no one is watching.

When you believe in yourself, anything is possible.

Instructions: Trace the sentence and then write it on your own.

A small act of kindness can make a big difference.

One kind word can change someone's whole day.

Stay curious, and never stop asking questions.

Instructions: Trace the sentence and then write it on your own.

A smile is the most powerful thing you can wear.

Every person has something special to offer the world.

Take one step at a time, and you will get there.

Instructions: Trace the sentence and then write it on your own.

Treat yourself and others with kindness and respect.

You have the power to create your own happiness.

Bravery is doing what is right, even when it's difficult.

Instructions: Trace the sentence and then write it on your own.

Every day is a chance to be better than yesterday.

You are never too young to make a difference.

Focus on progress, not perfection.

The only way to fail is to stop trying.

Instructions: Trace the sentence and then write it on your own.

Your potential is limitless.

The best way to learn is to try.

Be proud of how far you've come.

Comparison is the thief of joy.

SENTENCE SCRAMBLE

Instructions: Write the correct sentence neatly below each scrambled version.

• Scrambled: was yesterday The beautiful very sunset

• Correct: _____

• Scrambled: and ate baked dad a it cake My I chocolate

• Correct: _____

• Scrambled: because favorite nature My green I color is love

• Correct: _____

• Scrambled: couldn't fast believe I ran the rabbit how

• Correct: _____

SENTENCE SCRAMBLE

Instructions: Write the correct sentence neatly below each scrambled version.

- Scrambled: in the park played We afternoon this

- Correct: _____

- Scrambled: bike rode the hill My down cousin

- Correct: _____

- Scrambled: the won Our team game school

- Correct: _____

- Scrambled: a new book bought I yesterday

- Correct: _____

Instructions: Trace the sentence and then write it on your own.

Honey never spoils-you could eat honey that is thousands of years old.

The Eiffel Tower can grow taller in the summer because metal expands in heat.

Instructions: Trace the sentence and then write it on your own.

A group of flamingos is called a flamboyance.

Strawberries are the only fruits with their seeds on the outside.

A large cloud can hold millions of pounds of water.

Instructions: Trace the sentence and then write it on your own.

There are more stars in the universe than grains of sand on Earth.

A bolt of lightning can be five times hotter than the surface of the sun!

Instructions: Trace the sentence and then write it on your own.

Octopuses have three hearts and blue blood.

Your heart beats about 100,000 times a day.

Tigers have striped skin, not just striped fur.

Instructions: Trace the sentence and then write it on your own.

You cannot hum while holding your nose—try it.

There is an island in Japan filled with bunnies.

Some cats are allergic to humans.

The human brain cannot feel pain.

Instructions: Trace the sentence and then write it on your own.

The shortest war in history lasted only 38 to 45 minutes.

The world's largest snowflake on record was 15 inches wide.

Some turtles can breathe through their butts.

Instructions: Trace the sentence and then write it on your own.

The longest hiccuping spree lasted 68 years.

The world's largest desert is Antarctica, not the Sahara.

A single sneeze can travel up to 100 miles per hour.

Instructions: Trace the sentence and then write it on your own.

The inventor of the frisbee was turned into a frisbee after he died.

Squirrels plant thousands of trees every year by forgetting where they bury their acorns.

Instructions: Trace the sentence and then write it on your own.

A baby octopus is smaller than a grain of rice when it is born.

Sloths can hold their breath longer than dolphins.

The longest recorded flight of a chicken is 13 seconds.

Instructions: Trace the sentence and then write it on your own.

Cows have best friends and get sad when they are apart.

The human body has enough iron to make a small nail.

There is a volcano on Mars that is taller than Mount Everest.

Instructions: Trace the sentence and then write it on your own.

The blue whale's heart is the size of a small car.

The moon has moonquakes, just like earthquakes on Earth.

Snails can sleep for three years without waking up.

Instructions: Trace the sentence and then write it on your own.

A shrimp's heart is in its head.

The human brain is about 60% fat.

Kangaroos cannot walk backward.

Butterflies taste with their feet.

Instructions: Trace the sentence and then write it on your own.

If you could fold a piece of paper in half 42 times, it would be tall enough to reach the moon.

Pineapples take two years to grow before they are ready to eat.

Instructions: Trace the sentence and then write it on your own.

Hummingbirds are the only birds that can fly backward.

A day on Venus is longer than a year on Venus.

The speed of a sneeze is faster than a cheetah!

Instructions: Trace the sentence and then write it on your own.

The smell of freshly cut grass is actually a distress signal from the grass.

Some frogs can freeze solid in the winter and thaw out alive in the spring.

CREATIVE LETTERING CHALLENGE

Instructions: Write each of the words in all 4 different styles.

Happy

TALL & SKINNY

SHORT & WIDE

BUBBLE LETTERS

YOUR CREATIVE STYLE

Exciting

TALL & SKINNY

SHORT & WIDE

BUBBLE LETTERS

YOUR CREATIVE STYLE

Jump

TALL & SKINNY

SHORT & WIDE

BUBBLE LETTERS

YOUR CREATIVE STYLE

CREATIVE LETTERING CHALLENGE

Instructions: Write each of the words in all 4 different styles.

Giggle

TALL & SKINNY

SHORT & WIDE

BUBBLE LETTERS

YOUR CREATIVE STYLE

Amazing

TALL & SKINNY

SHORT & WIDE

BUBBLE LETTERS

YOUR CREATIVE STYLE

Imagine

TALL & SKINNY

SHORT & WIDE

BUBBLE LETTERS

YOUR CREATIVE STYLE

CREATIVE LETTERING CHALLENGE

Instructions: Write each of the words in all 4 different styles.

Dance

TALL & SKINNY	SHORT & WIDE

BUBBLE LETTERS	YOUR CREATIVE STYLE

Spin

TALL & SKINNY	SHORT & WIDE

BUBBLE LETTERS	YOUR CREATIVE STYLE

Bounce

TALL & SKINNY	SHORT & WIDE

BUBBLE LETTERS	YOUR CREATIVE STYLE

CREATIVE LETTERING CHALLENGE

Instructions: Write each of the words in all 4 different styles.

Zoom

TALL & SKINNY	SHORT & WIDE

BUBBLE LETTERS	YOUR CREATIVE STYLE

Sprint

TALL & SKINNY	SHORT & WIDE

BUBBLE LETTERS	YOUR CREATIVE STYLE

Flip

TALL & SKINNY	SHORT & WIDE

BUBBLE LETTERS	YOUR CREATIVE STYLE

CREATIVE LETTERING CHALLENGE

Instructions: Write each of the words in all 4 different styles.

Rocket

TALL & SKINNY	SHORT & WIDE

BUBBLE LETTERS	YOUR CREATIVE STYLE

Rainbow

TALL & SKINNY	SHORT & WIDE

BUBBLE LETTERS	YOUR CREATIVE STYLE

Dinosaur

TALL & SKINNY	SHORT & WIDE

BUBBLE LETTERS	YOUR CREATIVE STYLE

CREATIVE LETTERING CHALLENGE

Instructions: Write each of the words in all 4 different styles.

Puzzle

TALL & SKINNY	SHORT & WIDE
BUBBLE LETTERS	**YOUR CREATIVE STYLE**

Thunder

TALL & SKINNY	SHORT & WIDE
BUBBLE LETTERS	**YOUR CREATIVE STYLE**

Mystery

TALL & SKINNY	SHORT & WIDE
BUBBLE LETTERS	**YOUR CREATIVE STYLE**

CREATIVE LETTERING CHALLENGE

Instructions: Write each of the words in all 4 different styles.

Adventure

TALL & SKINNY

SHORT & WIDE

BUBBLE LETTERS

YOUR CREATIVE STYLE

Lightning

TALL & SKINNY

SHORT & WIDE

BUBBLE LETTERS

YOUR CREATIVE STYLE

Champion

TALL & SKINNY

SHORT & WIDE

BUBBLE LETTERS

YOUR CREATIVE STYLE

CREATIVE LETTERING CHALLENGE

Instructions: Write each of the words in all 4 different styles.

Invisible

TALL & SKINNY	SHORT & WIDE

BUBBLE LETTERS	YOUR CREATIVE STYLE

Celebration

TALL & SKINNY	SHORT & WIDE

BUBBLE LETTERS	YOUR CREATIVE STYLE

Exploration

TALL & SKINNY	SHORT & WIDE

BUBBLE LETTERS	YOUR CREATIVE STYLE

PRACTICAL WRITING APPLICATIONS

MY TO-DO LIST

Instructions: Imagine it's Saturday morning, and you have a busy day ahead! You need to complete chores, have some fun, and take care of personal tasks. **Write a to-do list with at least six tasks** you plan to complete today. Be specific—don't just write 'clean' but say **what** you need to clean. List your tasks in **order of importance**, with the most important ones at the top. **Check off each task as you complete it!**

- [ ] _____
- [ ] _____
- [ ] _____
- [ ] _____
- [ ] _____
- [ ] _____
- [ ] _____
- [ ] _____

GROCERY LIST

Instructions: Imagine you are helping your family plan meals for a big weekend! You need to make a grocery list that includes **breakfast, lunch, dinner, and dessert items**. Think about **foods you enjoy** and what ingredients you need for a complete meal. Write at least ten items on your list. Try to include a mix of **fruits, vegetables, proteins, snacks, and drinks!**

BREAKFAST

- [ ] _____
- [ ] _____
- [ ] _____

LUNCH

- [ ] _____
- [ ] _____
- [ ] _____

DINNER

- [ ] _____
- [ ] _____
- [ ] _____

DESSERT

- [ ] _____
- [ ] _____
- [ ] _____

DEAR FRIEND

Instructions: Write a **short letter to a friend or family member** about something exciting happening in your life. It could be about a **fun trip, a new hobby, or a school event**. Be sure to include:

• A **greeting** (Dear ___,).
• An **opening sentence** explaining why you're writing.
• 3-4 **sentences sharing details**.
• A **closing sentence** and a **friendly sign-off** (Sincerely, Your Friend, Love, etc.).

Date: _____

Dear _____

_____

_____

_____

_____

_____

_____

_____

YOU'RE INVITED!

Instructions: Imagine you are throwing an **awesome party**, and you need to invite your friends! Create an invitation that includes **all the important details**:

- **What the event is** (birthday, game night, movie night, etc.),
- The **date and time**.
- The **location**.
- **Any special instructions** (like what to bring or dress code).

Make it fun and exciting—**use words that make people want to come!**

Event Name: _____

_____

_____

_____

_____

_____

_____

_____

SHORT BIOGRAPHY

Instructions: Write a short biography about a person you **admire**—it could be a **family member, a historical figure, a scientist, an athlete, or someone famous**. Be sure to include:

- **Who they are** and what they are known for.
- **Three important things about their life**.
- **Why you admire them**.
- Write at least **5 sentences,** and make sure to explain **why this person is inspiring to you!**

Who They Are: _____

_____

_____

What They Did: _____

_____

_____

_____

_____

Why They Inspire Me: _____

_____

_____

HOW TO GET THERE

Instructions: Imagine you are giving directions to **a friend who has never been to your house**. Start from a familiar place (like a school, a park, or a store) and give **clear, step-by-step** directions to reach your house. Use words like:

- **Turn left/right.**
- **Go straight for ___ blocks.**
- 3-4 **sentences sharing details**.
- **Look for landmarks like a big tree or a red mailbox.**

Your directions should have **at least five steps** so that your friend does not get lost!

_____

_____

_____

_____

_____

_____

_____

Draw a map.

AMAZING PRODUCT ADVERTISEMENT

Instructions: Imagine you have invented **an amazing new product!** Write a short advertisement to **convince people to buy it.**

- Give your product a name.
- Describe what it does.
- Explain why people need it.
- Include a catchy slogan.

Make it sound exciting and fun!

Product Name: _____

What It Does: _____
_____
_____

Why You Need It: _____
_____

_____
_____

Draw a product.

Slogan: _____

FILLING OUT A SIMPLE FORM

Instructions: Imagine you are signing up for a **cool new club!** Fill out the form below with your information so they know more about you!

Name: _____

Age: _____

Favorite Hobby: _____

Favorite Food: _____

Why I Want to Join: _____

_____

_____

_____

_____

_____

_____

_____

TODAY'S WEATHER REPORT

Instructions: Imagine you are a **weather reporter on TV!** Write a **short weather report** for today's forecast. Be sure to include:

- The temperature.
- Whether it's sunny, cloudy, rainy, etc.
- What kind of clothing people should wear.
- Any fun weather facts!

_____

_____

_____

_____

_____

_____

_____

_____

_____

MY MOVIE/TV SHOW REVIEW

Instructions: Write a short review of **a movie or TV show** you love! Include:

- Title of the movie/show.
- A short summary (no spoilers!).
- What you liked best about it.
- Would you recommend it? Why or why not?

_____

_____

_____

_____

_____

_____

_____

_____

_____

_____

BREAKING NEWS

Instructions: Imagine you are a newspaper reporter writing about an exciting event! Your job is to create a **catchy headline** and a short news article blurb (3-4 sentences) that makes people want to read more. The event can be something fun like a **new roller coaster opening, a school talent show, a big sports win, or even a wild animal spotted in town!** Your article should include:

• A **headline** that grabs attention (Example: "Local Hero Saves Lost Puppy!").
• A **who, what, when, and where** in the first sentence.
• A short description with **one exciting detail** about the event.
• A **question or hint** that makes the reader want to know more!

Newspaper headline: _____

_____
_____
_____
_____
_____
_____
_____

SPEECH OR ANNOUNCEMENT

Instructions: Imagine you have to **make an announcement in front of a big audience!** Maybe you're the class president giving a speech, the **host of an award show**, or making a **big school announcement over the intercom**.

Your speech should include:

• Start with **an attention-grabbing first line** (Example: "Attention everyone! I have exciting news!").
• Explain **what you are announcing and why it matters.**
• End with a **call to action** (Example: "Don't forget to sign up by Friday!" or "Let's all work together to make this happen!").

_____
_____
_____
_____
_____
_____
_____
_____
_____

THE MYSTERIOUS BACKPACK

Instructions: Read the beginning of this story, then use your imagination to continue it! Make sure your handwriting is neat, and try to write at least five more sentences to finish the story.

When I opened my backpack this morning, I was shocked to find a tiny door inside. It had a little golden handle and a sign that said, "Do Not Open Until Lunchtime." I looked around to make sure no one was watching. Then I _____

_____

_____

_____

_____

_____

_____

_____

THE DISAPPEARING HOMEWORK

Instructions: Read the beginning of this story, then use your imagination to continue it! Make sure your handwriting is neat, and try to write at least five more sentences to finish the story.

I was about to turn in my homework when I realized it was gone! I checked my desk, my backpack, even under my chair—but it had completely disappeared. Then I noticed a tiny trail of pencil shavings leading toward the classroom window. _____

_____

_____

_____

_____

_____

_____

THE DAY IT RAINED POPCORN

Instructions: Read the beginning of this story, then use your imagination to continue it! Make sure your handwriting is neat, and try to write at least five more sentences to finish the story.

At first, I thought I was imagining it. But when I looked outside, I saw popcorn falling from the sky! People were running around with buckets, trying to catch it. My best friend grabbed a handful and said, "This is the best day ever!" But then, something even stranger happened, _____

_____

_____

_____

_____

_____

_____

_____

A SECRET DOOR IN THE LIBRARY

Instructions: Read the beginning of this story, then use your imagination to continue it! Make sure your handwriting is neat, and try to write at least five more sentences to finish the story.

I was looking for a book in the school library when I leaned against the bookshelf—and it swung open like a secret door! Behind it was a dark tunnel with a glowing light at the end. I took a deep breath, stepped inside, and _____

_____

_____

_____

_____

_____

_____

_____

MY PET'S SECRET TALENT

Instructions: Read the beginning of this story, then use your imagination to continue it! Make sure your handwriting is neat, and try to write at least five more sentences to finish the story.

I always knew my dog was smart, but I had no idea she could talk! This morning, as I was feeding her, she looked up at me and said, "About time! I've been waiting for breakfast forever." I nearly fell over. Then I said _____

_____

_____

_____

_____

_____

_____

_____

THE MYSTERY OF THE MISSING ICE CREAM

Instructions: Read the beginning of this story, then use your imagination to continue it! Make sure your handwriting is neat, and try to write at least five more sentences to finish the story.

My favorite ice cream was in the freezer last night. But when I went to get it today, it was gone! The only clue was a sticky spoon left on the counter. My family says they didn't take it, but someone must have! I grabbed a notepad and decided to solve the case. _____

_____

_____

_____

_____

_____

_____

_____

WRITING PROMPTS

IF YOU COULD HAVE ANY SUPERPOWER

If you could have any superpower, what would it be and why? Would you use it to help people, have fun, or do something else? Describe what your superpower does, how you would use it, and any challenges that might come with it. What would your superhero name be? Would you have a costume? Be as creative as possible!

A MYSTERIOUS DOOR APPEARS

One day, while walking home from school, you notice a mysterious door in the middle of your path. It wasn't there before! You take a deep breath and decide to open it. What do you see inside? Where does it lead? What happens when you step through? Describe everything in detail!

IF YOU COULD VISIT ANY TIME IN HISTORY

Imagine you have a time machine that can take you anywhere in history. Would you visit the past or the future? Would you meet someone famous or see an important event? Describe where and when you go, what you see, and what happens when you arrive!

THE DAY ANIMALS STARTED TALKING

You wake up one morning, and something incredible has happened—animals can talk! Suddenly, your pet (or a wild animal) starts having a conversation with you. What do they say? What do they think about humans? Do they have a secret life you never knew about? Write a story about this unusual day!

A NEW PLANET HAS BEEN DISCOVERED!

NASA just announced the discovery of a brand-new planet, and you get to name it! Describe what this planet looks like—what kind of land, oceans, or creatures does it have? Is it a place where humans could live? Does it have strange weather, floating cities, or crazy new technology? Be as creative as possible!

YOUR DREAM AMUSEMENT PARK

You have been chosen to design the ultimate amusement park! What is it called? What rides, games, and attractions does it have? Is it based on a theme (space, superheroes, dinosaurs)? Describe the coolest things visitors can do there and what makes it different from any other amusement park in the world!

IF YOU COULD SWITCH LIVES WITH A BOOK OR MOVIE CHARACTER

For one day, you get to switch lives with any character from a book or movie! Who would you choose? What would it be like to live in their world? Would you enjoy it, or would it be harder than it looks? Describe your day in their shoes!

THE BEST INVENTION EVER!

You have invented something that will change the world! What is it, and how does it work? Does it solve a big problem or make life more fun? Who would use it, and how would it help people? Write about why your invention is the greatest thing ever created!

CERTIFICATE OF COMPLETION

This Certificate of Completion
is presented to:

_____

for successfully completing
Print Handwriting Workbook

_____   _____
Date   Signature

We Appreciate You!

Thank you for working through this book—we hope it was a helpful and enjoyable learning experience! We put a lot of care into creating books that make learning fun and effective, and it means the world to us that you chose BrainWave Books.

Since we're a small, independent brand, your thoughts matter more than you know. If you have any feedback—big or small—we'd love to hear from you. **Your input helps us continue improving and creating the best learning materials possible.** Want to share your thoughts? Scan the QR code below.

Thanks again for being part of the BrainWave Books family! Keep learning, keep growing, and we hope to see you again in another one of our books.

— The BrainWave Books Team